my friend is struggling with . . .

Past Sexual Abuse

Josh McDowell
& Ed Stewart

WORD PUBLISHING

NASHVILLE

A Thomas Nelson Company

Scripture quotations used in this book are from the Holy Bible, New International Version. Copyright © 1973, 1978, 1984, International Bible Society. Used by permission of Zondervan Bible Publishers.

Library of Congress Cataloging-in-Publication Data

McDowell, Josh.
    My friend is struggling with—past sexual abuse / by Josh McDowell and Ed Stewart.
    p. cm. — (Project 911 collection)
    Summary: Uses the story of a teenage girl who was sexually abused by her grandfather to deal with issues related to sexual abuse and how to handle them from a Christian perspective.
    ISBN 0-8499-3797-3
    1. Sexually abused teenagers—Juvenile literature. 2. Sexually abused teenagers—Religious life—Juvenile literature. 3. Child sexual abuse—Juvenile literature. [1. Child sexual abuse. 2. Christian life.] I. Stewart, Ed. II. Title. III. Series.
    HV6570 .M39 2000
    362.76—dc21

          00-028109
          CIP

Printed in the United States of America

00 01 02 03 04 05 QDT 9 8 7 6 5 4 3 2 1

Acknowledgments

We would like to thank the following people:

David Ferguson, director of Intimate Life Ministries of Austin, Texas, has made a tremendous contribution to this collection. David's influence, along with the principles of the Intimate Life message, is felt throughout each book in this collection. David has modeled before us how to be God's comfort, support, and encouragement to others. We encourage you to take advantage of the seminars and resources that Intimate Life Ministries offers. (See pages 49–54 for more information about how this ministry can serve you.)

Dave Bellis, my (Josh) associate of twenty-three years, who labored with us to mold and

acknowledgments

shape each book in this collection. Each fictional story in all eight books of the PROJECT 911 collection was derived from the dramatic audio segments of the "Youth in Crisis Resource," which Dave personally wrote. He was also responsible for the design and coordination of the entire PROJECT 911 family of resources (see pages 55–58). We are so very grateful for Dave's talents and involvement.

Joey Paul of Word Publishing not only believed in this entire project, but also consistently championed it throughout Word.

JOSH MCDOWELL
ED STEWART

Ann's Story

The little girl stiffened with fear as she heard soft footsteps coming down the hall. Alone in her grandparents' darkened guest bedroom, she thought about slipping out of the bed and hiding beneath it. But hearing the doorknob slowly turn, she knew it was too late. So she pulled the covers over her head and burrowed to the bottom of the bed, hoping somehow he wouldn't find her.

She heard him step into the room. "Pumpkin, it's me, Grandpa," she heard him whisper. "Grandma is sound asleep, so we can have our secret visit now." The little girl squeezed herself into a tight ball at the bottom of the bed, wishing she could make herself smaller, wishing she could even disappear. She didn't like Grandpa's "secret visits." He touched her where she didn't like being touched. But she couldn't tell anyone about the touching because Grandpa said it was a secret. Besides, she didn't want to tell anyone because she thought she would get in trouble for doing such a bad thing.

The little girl heard the bedroom door close. "Come on out, Pumpkin," Grandpa whispered. She cringed as her grandfather's hands patted the covers until he found the lump at the bottom.

"No secret visit, Grandpa," she said as he began slowly peeling away the covers. "Please, Grandpa, no visit tonight."

"But we must have our secret visit, Pumpkin," he said in a syrupy tone. His hands were reaching between the sheets to find her.

She balled up as tightly as she could. "No, Grandpa, no. No, Grandpa, no. No, no—"

"Wake up, wake up." Ann felt someone jostling her gently by the shoulder. "You're having a nightmare, Annie. Wake up." The whispering voice she heard was not her grandfather's. It sounded like Heather's voice.

After another jostle, Ann snapped fully awake

with a start. Heather was shaking her, and it was dark. Ann suddenly remembered she was in a sleeping bag in her bunk at summer church camp. Heather and four other girls from church were in the cabin with her. Their adult counselor, Jenny Shaw, was there too.

Ann released a sigh of relief. She was not six years old as she'd been in her terrible dream; she was fourteen now. And she was not with her grandfather; she was with her friends at camp. Yet the dream had left her heart beating rapidly, and she was drenched with sweat even in the cool, rustic mountain cabin.

"Ann, are you all right?" Heather whispered. "You were saying, 'No, Grandpa, no.' It sounded like you were in pain."

Ann could barely make out her friend's face in the darkness. "Yeah, I'm all right," she said, just above a whisper. "Like you said, it was just a bad dream. I'm fine now."

Heather continued in a hushed tone. "It sounded awful, like your grandfather was chasing you with an ax or something."

"I'm sorry I woke you up," Ann said, diverting

3

attention from the dream. "I hope I didn't wake up the whole cabin."

"Don't worry," Heather assured her, "everybody else is still sawing logs."

Ann Cassidy considered Heather Wells the best of all possible friends. Heather had been like a sister—always there for her, always concerned. Their friendship had begun in the fifth grade when Ann's mother had enrolled her in Faith Christian School. Ann had thought it odd when Mom put her in a Christian school, especially since the family did not attend church. But it worked out for the best.

In that first year at Faith, Ann met two people who became very special to her. First, she met Heather Wells in Mr. Trotter's fifth-grade class. Second, she met Jesus Christ through the worship and Bible teaching in the weekly chapel service. Ann trusted Christ in October of that first year and began attending church with Heather on Sundays. They had been like sisters ever since.

"So what were you dreaming about?" Heather pressed with sisterly nosiness.

Ann didn't want to answer her. She'd had the same dream many times before. It always left her feeling dirty and empty, because she knew it was more than a bad dream. It was also a bad memory.

"It was nothing, really," Ann said, aware that she was seriously stretching the truth. "We should go back to sleep."

"Are you having problems with your grandfather, Annie?" Heather bored in, still whispering. "Is there something you want me to pray about?"

That was one of the many things Ann appreciated about Heather. Her friend prayed about everything. "Grandpa Bennett died two years ago," Ann answered.

"Oh, sorry. I just thought . . ." Her words trailed off.

"No problem," Ann said. "Let's get back to sleep. Are we still having morning devotions together?"

"Of course. Out by the archery range right after breakfast."

"Okay, good night," Ann whispered. "And thanks."

"Good night."

Ann was still awake when she heard deep, noisy breaths coming from the bunk next to hers. Heather had fallen back to sleep. *I didn't exactly tell you the truth, Heather,* Ann explained silently. *I don't have any problems with Grandpa now, because he's dead. But I have never told anyone about what Grandpa did to me. Now I'm so ashamed about what happened that I'm afraid to tell anyone. And I can't seem to get these awful memories to go away. Maybe it is something I need you to pray with me about.*

At breakfast, Jenny Shaw's cabin won the Camp Director's "Mr. Clean" award for the third straight day. Heather Wells led the raucous cheers—as usual—while Ann stayed in the background—as usual. Most people couldn't believe that she and Heather were friends. Heather was so outgoing and Ann was so quiet. And yet Heather never left Ann out of anything. It was another reason why Ann appreciated her best friend.

After breakfast, Ann and Heather went to their favorite log next to the archery range for devotions. Before they could open their Bibles,

Ann brought up the topic that had been in the front of her brain since their brief, middle-of-the-night chat. "Before we read, I have to apologize to you."

Heather cocked her head with curiosity. "For what?"

Ann squirmed on the log, feeling very nervous about bringing up the subject. "Last night I told you that I didn't have any problems with my grandpa."

"Yes, because your grandfather died two years ago."

"Well, I didn't exactly tell you the truth about Grandpa."

"You mean about him being dead?"

"No, I mean about the problems."

"You had problems with your grandfather? That's what the dream was about last night?"

The fresh reminder about the dream sent an icy chill down Ann's spine. She stared at the ground, pushing pine needles around with the toe of her sandal. Finally she said, "I've never told anyone about this, Heather, not even my parents."

Heather took Ann's hand. She seemed to sense how difficult it was for Ann to talk about it. "It's okay, Annie," she assured her. "You know I'm here for you. You can tell me if you want to."

"It all started when I was about four years old. My parents used to take me to stay with Grandma and Grandpa Bennett several weekends a year while they went away. When Grandma was asleep or at the store, my grandpa . . . did things to me . . . that weren't right." Ann could not keep tears of shame from flooding her eyes. "He . . . touched me in my private areas. He made me . . . touch him too. He said it was our secret. He said I should never tell anyone, so I never did. But I can't stop dreaming about it."

Resting her head on her friend's shoulder, Ann began to cry. She felt Heather's comforting arm around her and heard her sniffling too. "Annie, you poor thing," Heather said in a broken voice. "I didn't know you had such a big hurt in your past. I'm so sorry." The two of them sat and cried for another minute.

"How long did this go on?" Heather said as they wiped their eyes dry.

"About three years," Ann explained. "Then Grandpa got real sick. He was in a nursing home until he died two years ago.

"I didn't tell my parents," Ann continued, "because I thought I would get in trouble. I thought it was my fault."

"Annie, you were only a little kid," Heather argued. "It wasn't your fault. Your grandfather was wrong. Nobody should do those things to a little kid."

"Then why do I feel so guilty about what happened?"

Heather thought for a moment. "I don't know how to answer that, but maybe Jenny would." Jenny Shaw was their counselor at camp this week. Jenny and her husband, Doug, were volunteer youth leaders at the church Ann and Heather attended. Both girls thought of Jenny as a spiritual big sister.

"I don't know if I can tell Jenny about this," Ann said, frowning at the thought.

"I'm glad you told me about your dreams and your grandfather, Annie," Heather assured her. "I'm going to be with you and pray with you through this. But I think it would be good to ask Jenny's advice about how to handle all this. We could talk to her together."

Ann winced, but somehow she knew Heather was right. Jenny Shaw had been a great source of spiritual strength since she came into the youth group. "Maybe Jenny won't have time to talk," Ann argued weakly.

"You just tell me that you're ready to talk to her," Heather said, "and I'll do the rest."

As difficult as it had been for her to tell Heather her dark secret, Ann already felt better for doing so. It was as if Heather had taken some of the burden just by listening to her and crying with her. If talking to Jenny could help her feel even better, Ann could do it. "Okay," she said, "I'd like to talk to Jenny—if you'll go with me."

Heather smiled an encouraging smile. "You got it. That's what friends are for."

Heather asked Jenny to meet with them during free time right after lunch, and she agreed. They met in the cabin while their four roommates were horseback riding.

With Heather holding her hand for encouragement, Ann told Jenny about her dreams and the dark events from her childhood that inspired them. Jenny asked her all the who, where, and when questions without pushing her to go into sordid details. Ann couldn't keep from crying as she talked, but Heather and Jenny were right there for her. "It's okay to cry, Ann," Jenny encouraged, holding her. "Just let it all out. We're here for you." The tears flowed freely for all three of them.

When the emotions subsided, Jenny said, "There is a term for what happened to you during those 'secret visits' with your grandfather. Do you know what it is, Ann?"

Ann knew what Jenny was getting at. But she hesitated because it sounded so dirty, so terrible. "Yes, I know," she admitted finally.

"Then tell me what you'd call what your grandfather did to you during your secret visits," Jenny pressed.

They seemed like forbidden words to Ann, just like swearing or using God's name in vain. She didn't want to say them. But with Jenny's gentle prodding, she did. "Grandpa . . . sexually abused me."

"That's right, Ann," Jenny affirmed. "It's very important that you understand that. Parents and grandparents and other adults are supposed to care for you and protect you. No matter how loving he may have seemed at other times, your grandfather took something from you for his own pleasure, and that's abuse. Sexual abuse is a crime, Ann. If your grandfather were still alive and abusing you like that today, I would insist that you go to the police or a child-protection agency. It's that serious."

"But it seemed partly my fault," Ann interjected, fighting back tears again. "Grandpa used to say I was too cute to resist."

Jenny slowly shook her head. "It was not your fault, Ann. No matter what he told you, no matter how guilty it made you feel, you are not to blame."

Ann felt something very freeing in Jenny's words, as if another large weight had been lifted from her shoulders. "It wasn't my fault," she repeated.

"That's right," Jenny said, smiling. "And I also want you to know that I am proud of you for the courage it takes to face all this. And I want to help you heal from the terrible inner wound you suffered."

"Heal?" Ann wondered aloud. "But it was such a long time ago."

"Let me explain," Jenny said. "Suppose you broke your arm but never told anybody about it and never went to the doctor to get it set. What would happen?"

"The arm would probably get better, but it might be crooked," Ann guessed. "Or it might not get better at all."

"You're right," Jenny said. "And something like that has happened to you. You were emotionally wounded as a child because of your grandfather's abuse. Your emotions may have healed a little with time. But now God can involve others who care about you to help mend the emotional part of you that has been hurting for so long."

It made sense to Ann. "I see," she said.

"So I want you to know that I'm going to be with you as the healing takes place. You can count on me, Ann."

"Me too," Heather chimed in.

Jenny glanced at her watch. "But it's time for

13

team games down on the field right now. I would like to meet here again tomorrow if you two are willing. There are some other things about your abuse we need to talk about."

"I'd like that," Ann said eagerly. Heather agreed to be there too.

Before leaving the cabin, Jenny led the girls in a tender prayer for Ann's healing. All through the day Ann felt brighter and happier inside. She had revealed the darkest blot from her past, and two people who meant the world to her still loved her. Ann sensed that today was the beginning of a new chapter in her life.

Time Out to Consider

Sadly, Ann Cassidy's childhood experience with her grandfather is not isolated or unusual. It is estimated that a child is molested in this country every two minutes. Approximately one out of every three women and one out of every seven men have been sexually abused before the age of eighteen. The sexual abuse of children and adolescents may be invisible to many, but people like Ann who are the

14

victims of abuse know the pain, shame, and guilt it brings. You may be reading this booklet now because you also are the victim of sexual abuse.

Let's be sure we understand this term. Sexual abuse is any form of sexual activity or talk in which an adult seeks sexual gratification from a child. To be more specific, you have been sexually abused if any of the following have happened to you as a child or adolescent:

- An adult showed you his or her genitals.

- An adult asked you to undress in order to look at you or fondle you (touch you sexually).

- An adult touched your genitals or made you touch his or her genitals.

- An adult contacted your genitals with his or her mouth or made you contact his or her genitals with your mouth.

- An adult forced you to masturbate or to watch as he or she masturbated.

- An adult penetrated your anus or vagina with fingers, penis, or another object.

- An adult made you perform intercourse with him or her.

- An adult used you for the production of pornographic materials.

God hates sexual abuse. He created sex to be an act of mutual love between a husband and wife (see Gen. 2:24; Heb. 13:4). Any sexual activity outside this boundary is a violation of His will and design. This certainly includes an adult using a child for sexual gratification, as "innocent" as some adults may try to make their wrong behavior appear.

Sexual abuse distorts your understanding of sex and its wholesome purpose in God's design. Sexual abuse disrupts your normal process of emotional, social, and sexual maturity. Sexual abuse confuses you about the meaning of true human love and God's love. Sexual abuse violates you as an individual created in the image of God. If you are the victim of some kind of sexual abuse, you have been wounded emotionally and possibly physically by a selfish adult.

What are the effects of sexual abuse on children and adolescents? You may identify with one or more of the common effects mentioned below.

Physical illness and injury. The abuse Ann suffered from her grandfather did not harm her physically in a long-term way. Other children are not as fortunate. Some victims contract AIDS or other sexually transmitted diseases through contact with a promiscuous adult. Some suffer severe tissue tears due to penetration of the vagina or anus. Many illnesses and injuries from sexual abuse are permanent, and some are fatal.

Pregnancy. Some girls bear children as a result of sexual abuse, further complicating their already troubled lives.

False guilt. Why does Ann believe that her grandfather's abuse was at least partially her fault? Most young children view adults as perfect and just. If an adult does something to hurt them in some way, including sexually abusing them, the child may assume he or she has done something to deserve it. Other children feel false guilt or condemnation because they knew the abuse was wrong, but they could do nothing to stop it.

Shame. Shame is a cousin to condemnation. It is how you feel about the abusive acts in which you participated. Shame is how you feel about yourself. You may feel dirty, bad, worthless, or sinful as a result of being abused, even though it is not your fault.

Helplessness. When Ann was being sexually abused by her grandfather, she felt helplessly trapped in the "secret" they alone shared. She knew it was wrong, but she could not tell anyone. You may have been strongly encouraged, threatened, or perhaps bribed into silence by your abuser. Or you may have felt helpless because you tried to tell someone about the abuse and they ignored you or didn't believe you.

Poor sense of worth. Because they were treated disrespectfully and unkindly by their abusers, many victims are convinced that they are unloved, unlovable, and unworthy of love. They may find it difficult to believe that anyone else could love them, including God, a boyfriend or girlfriend, a parent, or a spouse. A poor sense of worth may lead to other emotional problems, such as eating disorders and thoughts of suicide.

More sexual abuse. Many victims of childhood sexual abuse are likely to be victimized again. Having lost a sense of worth from someone abusing them during the first experience, victims can begin to believe that they deserve other sexual abuse.

There are a number of other effects that stem from sexual abuse: aggression toward others, distrust of others, poor social skills, emotional withdrawal, running away, criminal behaviors (such as prostitution), depression, anger, fear, anxiety, and suicidal tendencies. As the victim of sexual abuse, you likely have been emotionally injured in one or more of these ways. You need the loving help of others to be healed. If you have kept your abuse a secret, as Ann did, or have not sought the help and counsel of others, now is the time to speak up and get the help you need.

As Ann discovered, it is incredibly painful and difficult to cope with the memory of sexual abuse. There are a couple of things to notice from the first part of Ann's story that may be helpful as you face the pain of your own sexual abuse.

First, you may experience a wide range of

emotions as you recall the pain of your experience. Like Ann, you may feel false guilt, shame, hopelessness, and even anger because of what happened to you. You may cry like you have never cried in your life when you first admit to being abused. You may feel emotionally drained and exhausted. And you may get intensely angry at the situation, at the person who abused you, at the person(s) you think should have protected you (a parent, an older sibling, etc.), or even at God for allowing it to happen.

It is important to understand that all these feelings are normal and natural. It is the way God wired you. Your emotions are a built-in release valve to help you handle the deep inner pain. Of course, there are both productive and unproductive ways of expressing these emotions.

Jenny Shaw's simple advice to Ann was sound. She encouraged her not to bottle up her feelings, but to let her grief flow out. Jenny said she was there to hurt with Ann and to cry with her. This response reflects Jesus' words in Matthew 5:4: "Blessed are those who mourn, for they will be comforted." Mourning is the process of getting the hurt out. You admit how bad you feel and let your tears flow so others can share your pain and weep with you. This is God's design for blessing you and beginning to heal the deep pain that accompanies a painful experience. It is good and necessary that you experience the different emotions that come at this time.

Second, your greatest need as you begin to deal with the pain of sexual abuse is for others to comfort you. That's why Jenny Shaw and Heather Wells surrounded Ann with hugs and tears. In a time of deep sorrow, our greatest comfort comes when others sorrow with us. One major way God shares His comfort with us is through other people. The apostle Paul wrote, "God . . . comforts us in all our troubles, so that we can comfort those in any trouble with the comfort we ourselves have received from God" (2 Cor. 1:3, 4).

What is comfort? Maybe it will help to see first what comfort is *not*. Comfort is not a "pep talk" urging you to hang in there, tough it out, or hold it together. Comfort is not an attempt to explain why bad things happen to people. Comfort is not a bunch of positive words about God being in

21

control and everything being okay. All of these things may be good and useful in time, but they do not fill our primary need for comfort.

People comfort us primarily by feeling our hurt and sorrowing with us. Jesus illustrated the ministry of comfort when His friend Lazarus died (see John 11). When Jesus arrived at the home of Lazarus's sisters, Mary and Martha, He wept with them (see vv. 33–35). His response is especially interesting in light of what He did next: raise Lazarus from the dead (see vv. 38–44).

Why didn't Jesus simply tell the grieving Mary and Martha, "No need to cry, My friends, because in a few minutes Lazarus will be alive again"? Because at that moment they needed someone to identify with their hurt. Jesus met Mary's and Martha's need for comfort by sharing in their sorrow and tears. Later He performed the miracle that turned their sorrow to joy.

We receive comfort when we know we are not suffering alone. Paul instructed us, "Rejoice with those who rejoice; mourn with those who mourn" (Rom. 12:15). When you experience sorrow, people may try to comfort you by cheering you up, urging you to be strong, or trying to explain away the tragic event. These people no doubt care about you and mean well by their words. But they may not know what comfort sounds like. Hopefully, there will also be someone around like Jenny and Heather who will provide the comfort you need. You will sense God's care and concern for you as this someone hurts with you, sorrows with you, and weeps with you. Jenny and Heather are good examples of what real comfort looks like in a painful circumstance.

But there is much more involved in healing the wounds caused by sexual abuse, as Ann Cassidy is about to discover.

Ann's Story

"Ann, what have you been thinking and feeling since our time yesterday?" Jenny Shaw was sitting on one bunk; Ann and Heather were on the bunk facing her. Their four roommates were down at the lake water-skiing and tubing.

"*Mixed* would be a good word," Ann said. "A

23

few bad flashbacks have popped into my mind without warning. And some of the old feelings came along with them—you know, feeling dirty, scared, ashamed. But at other times I thought about our talk yesterday and was really glad that somebody knows what I went through. I tried to push away the bad thoughts and feelings and concentrate on the good ones. A couple of times, when I felt like crying, I tried to think happy thoughts."

"Don't push away the hurtful stuff too hard, Ann," Jenny admonished in a loving tone. "One of the worst things you can do at this time is try to deny or forget what happened to you or to keep your emotions bottled up inside. Among the best things you can do is to face squarely what has happened, to recognize and express your feelings, and to accept the help of others. I think it would be good for you to see a Christian counselor if your parents will consent to it."

Ann felt an electric shock of fear. "My parents? You're not going to tell my parents about this, are you?"

Jenny reached out a hand to touch Ann gently on the arm. "It may be hard for you, but you need to tell your parents about the abuse. They are important to your healing."

"But what if Mom freaks out? Grandpa was her father."

"She will probably need comfort, support, and encouragement too," Jenny explained. "But she loves you, and I'm sure she wants to help you get through your pain, even if it's also painful for her."

Ann felt butterflies in her stomach. "How do I break this news to my parents?"

"We can talk about that before we go home on Saturday, Ann," Jenny assured her. "But I'll go with you when you tell them—if you want me to."

"I can be there, too, Annie," Heather put in, "if you need somebody to lean on."

Ann's butterflies didn't all go away, but they quieted down some. "You two would really go with me?"

"I'll be glad to be there for you," Jenny said.

"I don't want you to be alone during such a tough time," Heather added. "If you want me there, I'm there."

25

Ann felt a little teary again at the expression of Jenny's and Heather's closeness. "This isn't easy for me," she said. "I'll take all the help I can get."

Heather gave her a big hug.

Then Jenny said, "Ann, I want to encourage you to take advantage of your most important resource for handling everything you're dealing with right now. That resource is God Himself. I want you to know that God does not look down on you because you have been sexually abused. He knows it wasn't your fault. He's not disappointed or mad at you because of how you were treated by your grandfather. I want you to see how God really feels about you. Get your Bibles."

Ann and Heather pulled out their Bibles. Jenny gave each of them a verse to look up. "Ann, your verse tells us something about how God feels about your pain. Why don't you read Isaiah, chapter sixty-three, verse nine."

Ann read aloud. "'In all their distress he too was distressed, and the angel of his presence saved them. In his love and mercy he redeemed them; he lifted them up and carried them all the days of old.'"

"According to this verse, how does God feel when His people are distressed?" Jenny quizzed.

"He feels distressed too," Ann answered.

"So how do you think God feels about what you have been through, Ann?"

"I'm sad and upset about it, so I guess He's sad and upset with me."

Jenny leaned closer. "And how does that make you feel?"

Ann paused to think about it. "If He hurts because I'm hurting, it makes me feel very special, like He really knows me and loves me."

"That's right, Ann," Jenny emphasized. "He knows all about you. He knows how much pain your grandfather's abuse has caused over the years. And He hurts because you hurt. It will help you to remember that."

"My verse is really encouraging too," Heather said.

Jenny nodded. "Read Matthew chapter eleven, verse twenty-eight for us, Heather."

"'Come to me, all you who are weary and burdened, and I will give you rest.'"

Jenny looked at Ann. "Do you feel 'weary and

burdened' from the dark secret you have carried since your grandfather abused you?"

"That's one way to put it," Ann said.

"According to this verse, what does Jesus have to offer for your condition?"

Ann glanced at the verse in Heather's Bible then looked back at Jenny. "Rest," she answered with a slight smile.

"There's one more passage I want you to see, Ann." Jenny directed them to Hebrews 4:15–16.

Heather volunteered to read aloud while Ann followed along in her Bible. "'For we do not have a high priest who is unable to sympathize with our weaknesses, but we have one who has been tempted in every way, just as we are—yet was without sin. Let us then approach the throne of grace with confidence, so that we may receive mercy and find grace to help us in our time of need.'"

"God not only feels my hurt and offers rest, but He can also help me," Ann said.

"That's so important to understand, Ann," Jenny said. "God is willing and waiting to help you get through your tough time. So one of the

28

best things you can do to cope with your feelings is to cultivate a deeper relationship with God and depend on Him for strength and help."

Ann dropped her head. "I haven't been doing too well in that category. This helps me want to get back to having personal devotions again."

"That's good, Ann," Jenny responded. "Spending time each day in prayer and Bible reading will really help."

Before leaving the cabin for group games, Jenny and the girls talked about Ann setting up a time to tell her parents about the abuse she suffered. Jenny and Heather repeated their promise to be with Ann when she revealed her shocking news. It made Ann feel a little better, but she was still nervous about how her parents would react, especially her mother.

Ann secretly wished it were all over. She had finally confessed her dark secret to caring friends and felt much better for having received their comfort. Why couldn't she be completely healed from the pain right now? Jenny had told her it would be a process, and Ann realized she was probably right. After all, it took time to heal from a broken arm or from surgery. Why would it be different for inner hurts? The only good news about a process of healing was that she didn't have to go through it alone. Jenny and Heather would be at the top of her praise list for a long time to come.

Time Out to Consider

It is very common for someone like Ann who is coming to terms with sexual abuse in the past to grieve. Ann buried the deep pain of being violated physically, mentally, and emotionally as a child. Now that the incidents have come to light, the pain returns and she must grieve the loss of the sanctity of her body. The grieving process, which may continue for several weeks or months, has five clearly identifiable stages. No two people go through the process in exactly the same way, and the stages often overlap and recur. But if you are just coming to terms with sexual abuse, you will likely find yourself responding something like Ann did.

One of the first responses of grief is *denial.*

You may find yourself at times unwilling to believe that such a terrible thing happened to you. You may have been stuck in denial for years as you kept the abuse a secret. Ann displayed this response for several years as she resisted telling anyone what her grandfather did to her. One of the ways your mind and emotions will try to handle the shock of your grief is to say, "No way, this did not happen to me."

A second stage in responding to grief is *anger*. When grappling with the inevitable question, "Why did this happen?" you may find yourself lashing out angrily because there is no reasonable answer to that question. You have been violated and shamed, and it seems terribly unfair. You may be angry over the circumstances that led to the abuse, as Ann was at being forced to stay at her grandparents' home. You may feel anger toward the person who abused you. You may be angry at God for allowing it to happen. Your anger may even be directed at yourself because you suspect that you were somehow to blame for what happened.

A third stage of grief is *bargaining* with God

for relief from the awful event and its consequences. You may find yourself secretly trying to cut a deal with God, vowing to change your behavior if He will just take the pain and the memories away. You may be prompted to try to cut a deal with God both to change the circumstance and make up for your perceived failures.

Another stage of grief is *depression* when you realize that the past can never be changed. It's the feeling of overwhelming sadness or hopelessness over what happened to you. Depression may be accompanied by fear, anxiety, or insecurity about facing that person again. Intense loneliness is another facet of depression. You may want to isolate yourself from others in order to keep your past a secret. In doing so you will cut yourself off from the friends and loved ones who can help you.

The final stage of grief is *acceptance.* As time goes by and the other stages of grief diminish, you will be able to accept the reality of your abuse and begin to deal with it constructively. Even as this stage becomes dominant, you may still experience pangs of denial, anger, and depression. But they will be minimal compared to the more positive sense that God is working out your experience for good (see Rom. 8:28).

Christian counselors and leaders generally agree that it is normal and healthy to experience the five stages of grief following the traumatic events of sexual abuse. In many cases it takes many weeks or months to navigate successfully all five stages. Some of the emotions and thoughts that you experience during this time may be new to you or stronger than ever before in your life. You may wonder if there is something wrong with you for reacting in these ways. There is not. You are going through a common response to a very sad event in your life.

One of your best allies in dealing with the pain of sexual abuse is time. The old proverb "Time heals all wounds" contains a nugget of truth. Accept that fact that it will take time for you to get over your deep pain. You need time to process the jumble of feelings and thoughts. You need time to talk out your feelings with mature, compassionate Christian friends and perhaps a professional Christian counselor. As the weeks pass, your hurt will diminish and your life will return to a fairly normal pattern. Give time a chance to work for you by not expecting the pain and confusion to go away too soon.

When Ann poured out the story of being abused by her grandfather, Heather and then Jenny rallied around her with healing comfort. But she needed more than comfort to get through the pain of dealing with past abuse, and so do you. There are two more important elements that hopefully are being supplied to you.

First, you need the support of others. What's the difference between comfort and support? People supply the comfort you need when they share your sorrow emotionally. People supply the support you need by helping you during this time in practical, helpful ways. You need the help of people who are committed to obeying Galatians 6:2: "Carry each other's burdens, and in this way you will fulfill the law of Christ." For example, Jenny showed her practical support by counseling Ann and offering to go with her when she told her parents. Heather showed that she was a supportive friend by promising to stick with Ann through the healing process. Support is also provided when people volunteer to run errands for you, to help you with chores, or otherwise to ease your burden so you can concentrate on healing.

You may be tempted to ignore or to refuse the support offered by others. You may feel that you can handle everything yourself, or you may not want others to be bothered with things you normally do for yourself. Resist that temptation. God put Galatians 6:2 in the Bible because He knows there are times we should rely on the support of others. This is such a time. Let other people do things for you, and be grateful for their help. It is one of the ways God is providing for your needs at this time.

What if you have a need and nobody steps up to offer help? Ask for it. There is nothing wrong with telling a trusted friend, a youth leader, or your minister about your need and asking for help. For example, had Jenny and Heather not offered to go with Ann when she talked to her parents, she could have asked them to do so. In most cases, people are more than willing to help out; they just don't know what needs to be done.

Feel free to help people support you at this time by letting them know what you need.

Second, you need the encouragement of others. You receive encouragement when someone does something thoughtful to lift your spirits. Ann was encouraged whenever Jenny and Heather asked how she was doing. She was encouraged by their hugs and prayers. In the weeks and months ahead, she will receive their encouragement through cards, notes, and phone calls that communicated, "We're here for you." Encouraging deeds like these may not seem as practical as doing chores and running errands, but they are just as necessary.

Once again, if you do not receive the encouragement you need, ask for it. It's okay to tell someone who cares about you, "I need a hug" or "I just need you to be with me for a while."

The good advice Jenny shared with Ann about God's involvement in her life is appropriate for you as well. God is not offended by your abuse, nor does He disapprove of you because of what someone else did to you. He loves you, and your experience of being abused hurts Him too. He longs to show His compassion to you and ease your inner pain. And He is powerful enough to help you.

If you are not spending time daily in prayer and Bible reading, now is a good time to start. James 4:8 invites us, "Come near to God and he will come near to you." One of the ways to get close to God and allow Him to get close to you is through prayer and His Word. For example, start out by reading a psalm from the Bible each day. Then spend a few minutes telling God about what you are thinking and feeling. Ask Him to help you grow stronger through the healing process. He will do it because He loves you and wants to help you.

An important step in the process of healing from sexual abuse is telling your parents and enlisting their help in dealing with the pain. It may not be easy, but as Ann is about to discover, sharing openly with your parents will allow them fully to support the healing process.

Ann's Story

When Jenny Shaw arrived at the Cassidy home late Sunday afternoon, Ann introduced her to her parents, Jerry and Dorothy. Heather Wells was already there. Ann had told her parents only that Jenny wanted to chat with them about some topics that had come up at camp.

"We had a great time at camp, Mr. and Mrs. Cassidy," Jenny began. "And I really enjoyed being with your daughter and the other girls. Ann is a delightful girl, and I love her like a younger sister." Jerry and Dorothy beamed with pride.

"We hold summer camp each year to have a good time," Jenny continued. "But spending a week together also gives the girls an extended opportunity to talk about the more serious side of life, such as their struggles and problems. Don't worry: Ann isn't in any kind of trouble. But last week she talked to me—along with Heather—about something very hurtful in her life. I've encouraged her to share it with you. Heather and I are here mainly to provide moral support. Go ahead, Ann."

Ann wanted to roll up into a ball and hide, just as she had when her grandfather had come into her room at night years ago. Jenny encouraged her to go ahead even though she was nervous. So she took a deep breath and began. "Mom and Dad, do you remember the times you left me at Grandpa and Grandma Bennett's when you went away for weekends?"

Jerry nodded, and Dorothy said, "Yes, your grandparents always loved having you come over. It was just before Grandpa got sick. You were about five or six at the time."

Ann forced herself to go on. "Well, something happened while I was staying with them. It happened several times, and I never told you about it." Ann paused and bit her lip. "I . . . I was sexually abused by Grandpa Bennett."

The expression of shock on her parents' faces was severe. "What?" her dad retorted in disbelief.

Ann remembered Jenny urging her to state clearly what had happened. "For about three years, Grandpa Bennett sexually abused me when I stayed at their house. He made me keep it a secret."

Ann glanced at her mother just as the woman began to dissolve into tears. Clasping a hand to her mouth, she said repeatedly, "Oh no, oh no." Ann's father seemed to have turned to stone—a look of horror etched on his face.

Ann pressed on. "I never told anyone about it because I was embarrassed and scared. But I have had nightmares about what happened ever since. At camp, I had another bad dream. So I told Heather and Jenny about the abuse. Jenny said I should tell you, even though we knew it would be hard. I really need your help to get through this."

"I wish you had told us, Ann," Jerry said with sadness in his voice.

"I was afraid, Dad. I thought it was partly my fault, and I didn't want to get into trouble. Besides, Grandpa said it was our little secret, and I believed him."

Silence fell on the room like a suffocating blanket. Ann's mother cried softly, and her father sat in silence, stunned and hurt. Ann dabbed the tears from her eyes as she watched her parents process the shocking news. Heather and Jenny sat and prayed silently.

Finally, Jerry Cassidy got up from his chair and approached his daughter. Kneeling down in front of her, he said with tears spilling from his eyes, "Sweetheart, I'm so sorry I wasn't there to protect you. You didn't deserve to be abused. It wasn't your fault. I hurt so deeply for you because I love you so much." Then he enveloped Ann in his arms, and they sobbed together. In seconds, Dorothy joined them. Jenny and Heather watched while blinking away tears.

After a few minutes, Jenny stood and said, "I'm sure there are many things you want to talk about together, so we'll leave you alone. I suggested to Ann that the three of you consider seeing a Christian counselor together. Perhaps Pastor O'Neill can recommend someone in the community."

"That's a good idea," Jerry said, standing and wiping tears from his face with a handkerchief.

"You and Ann are going to need some time to heal from this deep emotional wound," Jenny continued. "Each of you will need all the comfort, support, and encouragement you can receive. Doug and I are available to help any way we can. And Ann is blessed to have a supportive friend like Heather. In time, I know God will help

Ann, and both of you, to heal from the awful things that happened."

Jenny led the small group in a brief prayer. Then she and Heather hugged the Cassidys good-bye. As they moved toward the door, Ann went with them. "Thank you so much for being here with me," she said. "I don't think I could have done it without you."

"We're just so happy that you were able to tell your horrible secret," Jenny said. Heather smiled and nodded in agreement.

"Just think," Ann said, "this probably wouldn't have happened if Heather hadn't been there when I had the nightmare. And you were right there, Jenny, when we needed to talk to you. I'm so glad God put you two in my life."

"We need one another," Jenny reminded her two young friends. "God designed us to function best when we have the comfort, support, and encouragement of others. He doesn't want us to hurt or to heal alone."

Ann smiled broadly. "Then I want to adopt you both as sisters so none of us are ever alone again." They laughed together, hugged once again, and then said good-bye.

Time Out to Consider

It is vitally important that you sit down with your parents as soon as possible to tell them about the sexual abuse you have suffered and begin to seek their help in your healing process. If the sexual abuser is one of your parents, tell your youth leader or other Christian adult who will give you guidance. Here are several steps that will help you prepare for and carry out such a meeting.

Decide if you want someone else to go with you. Ann was grateful to have the counsel and encouragement of her youth leader, Jenny Shaw. Perhaps you would feel more confident about the meeting with your parents if someone went with you. If you have shared your situation with someone like Jenny—a youth leader, a mature friend, or a minister—that person may be willing to go along when you talk to your parents.

Schedule a time to meet at their earliest convenience. Plan to talk to your parents or youth leader as soon as possible. Find a time and place for your meeting that will be free from interruptions and distractions. You might say to your parents, "I have something important I want to discuss with you. When could we sit down and talk?"

Be straightforward. Get right to the point. Either you or the "Jenny Shaw" who is with you should state clearly to your parents or youth leader that you are the victim of sexual abuse. Beating around the bush will only make your disclosure more painful for everyone.

Ask for their help. Express and explain your current thoughts about the healing process. Invite their counsel and prayers as you decide whether to seek Christian counseling. If the person who abused you is still alive, ask your parents or youth leader to help you report the abuse to the proper authorities to make sure the person will not abuse others.

Close with prayer. If your parents are Christians, ask them to join you in a time of prayer. Together ask God for His direction and help in the coming months as you begin to heal from the pain of your experience of sexual abuse.

As you convey respect for your parents' feelings and a willingness to listen to their concerns and suggestions, you increase the possibility that they will become your helpful supporters in the months ahead. Knowing that your dearest loved ones are on your side will help lift some of the emotional burden from your shoulders.

Four months after confessing the dark secret of sexual abuse and seeking help, Ann's life was turning around. The shyness that had plagued her since childhood was beginning to fade away. Instead of withdrawing around others, Ann became more self-confident and socially involved. As the condemnation, shame, and embarrassment disappeared, she was free to enjoy others and minister to their needs, just as Heather and Jenny had done for her. You can experience the same freedom from the pain of sexual abuse in your past. It all begins with these important first steps.

1. *Tell it like it is: You have been sexually abused.* You must clearly acknowledge to yourself and a trusted friend or counselor what happened to you. You must state what the experience has done to you without trying to explain it away. Once you get it out in the open, you will be able to start the healing process.

2. *Stop the abuse immediately.* If the abuse has not stopped, take immediate steps to stop it by notifying the police, a Christian minister or counselor, or a child-protection agency in your community. The "Jenny Shaw" in your life will likely be glad to help you take this step.

3. *Place the responsibility where it belongs.* Do not blame yourself for what someone else did to you. The person who abused you is solely responsible for his or her actions, no matter how that person tries to shift the blame to you. You are the victim. It was not your fault.

4. *Turn to God as the source of your healing.* Acknowledge that God did not cause the abuse but that He is the solution to the

trauma brought on by the abuse (see Ps. 18:2–6, 25–30).

5. *Allow yourself to grieve your loss of innocence.* A caring friend or adult can help you work through the denial, anger, bargaining, depression, and acceptance that will come from your loss. Instead of turning from such feelings, confront them, express them, and resolve them through the understanding and comfort of those who love you.

6. *Seek fellowship with God.* Pursue and maintain a daily appointment to be with God in prayer and Bible reading. Determine to rely on His strength, learn from His Word, and fight any destructive thoughts and feelings with the attitude of Christ (see Phil. 4:4–9).

7. *Seek the help of others.* Spend time with those who genuinely love you and desire to help you through the healing process: understanding parents, a youth leader or minister, a close friend, a Christian counselor, or a support group.

8. *Realize that healing will take time.* The process
    of healing from sexual abuse may be painful
    and take several weeks or months. But you
    survived the abuse; you can also overcome
    the trauma of recovery with God's help.

APPENDIX

Several times in this book I have mentioned the
work of Dr. David Ferguson. David's ministry
has had such a profound effect on me in the past
several years that I want you to have every opportunity to be exposed to his work and ministry.
David and his wife, Teresa, direct a ministry
called Intimate Life Ministries.

WHO AND WHAT IS INTIMATE LIFE MINISTRIES?
Intimate Life Ministries (ILM) is a training and
resource ministry whose purpose is to *assist in
the development of Great Commandment ministries worldwide.* Great Commandment ministries—ministries that help us love God and our
neighbors—are ongoing ministries that deepen

49

our intimacy with God and with others in marriage, family, and the church.

Intimate Life Ministries comprises:

- A network of **churches** seeking to fortify homes and communities with God's love;

- A network of **pastors and other ministry leaders** walking intimately with God and their families and seeking to live vulnerably before their people;

- A team of **accredited trainers** committed to helping churches establish ongoing Great Commandment ministries;

- A team of **professional associates** from ministry and other professional Christian backgrounds, assisting with research, training, and resource development;

- **Christian broadcasters, publishers, media, and other affiliates,** cooperating to see marriages and families reclaimed as divine relationships;

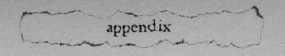

- **Headquarters staff** providing strategic planning, coordination, and support.

How Can Intimate Life Ministries Serve You?
ILM's Intimate Life Network of Churches is an effective, ongoing support and equipping relationship with churches and Christian leaders. There are at least four ways ILM can serve you:

1. *Ministering to Ministry Leaders*
ILM offers a unique two-day "Galatians 6:6" retreat to ministers and their spouses for personal renewal and for reestablishing and affirming ministry and family priorities. The conference accommodations and meals are provided as a gift to ministry leaders by cosponsoring partners. Thirty to forty such retreats are held throughout the U.S. and Europe each year.

2. *Partnering with Denominations and Other Ministries*
Numerous denominations and ministries have partnered with ILM by "commissioning" them to equip their ministry leaders through the

Galatians 6:6 retreats along with strategic training and ongoing resources. This unique partnership enables a denomination to use the expertise of ILM trainers and resources to perpetuate a movement of Great Commandment ministry at the local level. ILM also provides a crisis-support setting to which denominations may send ministers, couples, or families who are struggling in their relationships.

3. *Identifying, Training, and Equipping Lay Leaders*

ILM is committed to helping the church equip its lay leaders through:

- *Sermon Series* on several Great Commandment topics to help pastors communicate a vision for Great Commandment health as well as identify and cultivate a core lay leadership group.

- *Community Training Classes* that provide weekly or weekend training to church staff and lay leaders. Classes are delivered by Intimate

Life trainers along with ILM video-assisted training, workbooks, and study courses.

- *One-Day Training Conferences* on implementing Great Commandment ministry in the local church through marriage, parenting, or singles ministry. Conducted by Intimate Life trainers, these conferences are a great way to jump-start Great Commandment ministry in a local church.

4. *Providing Advanced Training and Crisis Support*

ILM conducts advanced training for both ministry staff and lay leaders through the Leadership Institute, focusing on relational ministry (marriage, parenting, families, singles, men, women, blended families, and counseling). The Enrichment Center provides support to relationships in crisis through Intensive Retreats for couples, families, and singles.

For more information on how you, your church, or your denomination can take advantage of the many services and resources, such as

the Great Commandment Ministry Training
Resource offered by Intimate Life Ministries,
write or call:

Intimate Life Ministries
P.O. Box 201808
Austin, TX 78720-1808
1-800-881-8008
www.ilmministries.com

Connecting Youth in Crisis

Obtain other vital topics from the PROJECT 911 Collection...

Experience the Connection

For Youth & Youth Groups

This eight-week youth group experience will teach your youth the true meaning of deepened friendships—being a 911 friend. Each lesson is built upon scriptural teachings that will both bond your group together and serve to draw others to Christ.

This optional video is an excellent supplement to your group's workbook experience.

As follow-up to your youth group experience, continue a young person's friendship journey by introducing them to a thirty-day topical devotional journal and a book on discovering God's will in their life.

Experience the Connection

For Adults & Groups

This watershed book is for parents, pastors, youth workers, or anyone interested in seeing youth not only survive but thrive in today's culture.

Book on Audio

This book, directed specifically to fathers, offers ten qualities to form deepened relationships between dads and their kids.

Begin your church-wide emphasis with an adult group experience using this five-part video series. Josh provides biblical insights for relationally connecting with your youth.

Experience the Connection

For Youth Workers

A one-on-one resource to help you provide a relational response and spiritual guidance to the 24 most troubling issues youth face today.

This handbook brings together over forty youth specialists to share their insights on what makes a successful youth ministry.

Contact your Christian supplier to obtain these PROJECT 911 resources and begin experiencing the connection God intended.